T0245003

Below
Zero

poems by
Carol V. Davis

STEPHEN F. AUSTIN STATE UNIVERSITY PRESS

For more information:
Stephen F. Austin State University Press
P.O. Box 13007 SFA Station
Nacogdoches, Texas 75962
sfapress@sfasu.edu
www.sfasu.edu/sfapress

Managing Editor: Kimberly Verhines
Book Design: Meredith Janning
Cover Art: Johanna Drucker
Distributed by Texas A&M Consortium
www.tamupress.com

ISBN: 978-1-62288-946-4

For my colleagues at Buryatia State University

Contents

❄

III.

❄

IV.

❄

"Such bliss that the snow is shining, that the cold has grown stronger"
Bella Akhmadulina

"Какое блаженство, что блещут снега, что холод окреп"
Белла Ахмадулина

I.

On Flying to Siberia for the First Time

It's true I was nervous.
It didn't help that my local travel agent instructed me
to buy the tickets in the U.S.... just in case.
Not exactly a believer, I hedged my bets, tucked
a copy of a sacred book, the *Tania*, in my carry-on
(the irony of a Lubavitcher rebbe exiled to Siberia a century before).
Packed the travel icon a friend gave me on my last trip to Russia.

I tried to block memory of a news video: a flight crew
scraping ice off the wings of a Tupolev-154 on a
Siberian runway, as routine as de-icing the windshield
of a car parked in an upstate driveway.

Shuffling in a long line at Gate 34, Sheremetyevo Airport:
Siberia Air, Flight 115, Moscow to Ulan-Ude, I eyed
the other passengers. I was the only American on board.
Squeezed near the last row between two thick Buryat men,
I gripped the armrests, as if they were the handlebars of a Harley,
the task of revving the engine for takeoff, mine alone.

An hour in, vast snowfields unfurled, pockmarked by
tiny villages spouting chimney smoke.
No seat vacant, the hum of conversation quieted,
the sky darkening, another five hours to go.
A mumble of Hebrew rose from my lips for a safe flight
and landing, that I be met on the other end,
that I would see my family again.

White Nights

Midnight could be noon, people strolling
on the Embankment unable or unwilling
to tell the difference. Drunken song and linked arms.
It is January I love, when night tucks into the corners
of the city with piles of snow pushed against the curb.
The blinking lights of the blini café, the samovar's
breath puffing against the front window.
Walking back from the metro, blackness presses against
the Soviet block apartments until they are indistinguishable.
Darkness untamed even in this major metropolis.
The day I took the wrong minibus, ended far from the city,
the fear of never getting back, picturing my wool coat
curled beneath the birches, a small animal.
Not that the bus left me so far out, but alone
on a road, past a half frozen lake, a shabby church
with a midnight cupola, no English in sight.
I crossed the road, stamped my feet to keep from numbing,
a prayer to keep my tongue from losing its agility.
A man pulled a sled piled with firewood on a path
that was no path.
I waited.

December

The apartment is warm again
after days without heat, a common occurrence,
even though the Russian government
is bloated with oil money.
Ice patterns return to the windows,
glide like skaters performing figure eights.
Clumps of snow gather into houses on the sills.
A face with wild hair appears one morning in the dark,
watches me cross the kitchen floor to put the kettle on.
Its eyes track me like the stony portrait on the stairs
of a palace confiscated after the Revolution.
Soon I will leave this city, stripped of its leaves
and hopes, while caricatures of mafia men
count their money, bribe officials and vacation offshore.
The metro steps are lined with old women
holding sweaters on hangers that sway
to forgotten Christmas songs.
No one looks at the display, nor stops to finger the goods.
The gold threads on the sleeves do not fool anyone.

Single Cell Scientist

At first when she asked for help with her scholarly paper,
I did not understand the words I translated, even though
they were in a language I know, but the Latin names
meant nothing: *prokaryote, eukarote, protist.*

*

Daylight was shrinking, the Neva River patched with ice.
November, two months into a year in Russia.
The sun disappearing under a mantle of gray.

*

Even with only one chromosome, the *prokaryotes*
can thrive in extreme environments.
Never having lived in a snowy climate would not be an obstacle.

*

The scientist invited me to her place of work, greeted me
on the icy sidewalk to usher me past guards stomping
against the cold by the entrance of the Zoological Museum
(a former palace like much of St. Petersburg).

*

Up and down dingy staircases, barely lit
(I'd never make it out on my own while my passport,
stored in a shoebox at the university, awaited registration.)

*

In the back of this 19th c. museum, she pushed open
a door heavy enough to withstand the storming of the Winter Palace.
Her office crammed with four others (anti-Semites, the scientist whispered).

*

She motioned me to her microscope, pushed a chair under me.
A rod-shaped *prokaryote* was doing laps back and forth over the glass slide.

Day Four, Ulan-Ude, Republic of Buryatia

The sky shifts from soot-colored
        to a noncommittal gray, a whispered sign
of dawn, the last day of the new year's holidays.
        Even at 9 a.m., few lights blink on
in the apartment building bordering the empty lot.

In the kindergarten across the street,
        a banner wishing
Happy New Year to a Beloved City,
        the only bright colors visible
this monochromatic morning.

Snow stacks on a stone wall outside the window
        layered like sheets of filo dough
but without the warmth of melted butter.
        An old man leans heavily on a cane
crossing what is perhaps a street

(no pavement visible), while a dog races past.
        In a hurry to get somewhere, I hope.
A woman trudges uphill in sealskin boots,
        a curl of smoke rising from the cigarette
held close to her face, aloft, an exclamation point

as if to remind winter that spring will come.
        I start to wonder what I am doing here.

On the Way to the Pushkin Hills

A blue-black bruise expanding. Night. Conversations shrink to staccato pricks row by row; two Americans hurtling into the Russian countryside wonder only briefly if the bus were to crash, would we ever be identified? Another village. Small curls of smoke. Carved window frames. Snow falls, mounds rise from the roadside, as if they will soon meet. Nearing midnight we slow down to enter a barely paved road through a dense forest. Branches scrape the roof. I half expect *Baba Yaga* to thrust from behind a trunk, stop the bus with a flick of her wrist. We pull beside a small wooden structure, more hostel than hotel, stumble out, bleary eyed. Light draws us in moth-like. We leave our passports at the desk and stumble upstairs. The room bare as a monk's cell. I peer out the window at white stripes of birch trees. This country so vast, we so far from anywhere. A young couple, newlyweds we are told, step out the front door. Fur tight against her neck, she raises an arm to light a cigarette, its tip red as a fox's eyes against the night.

Nursery Rhyme

A life is not a recollection of facts
Charles Baxter

I did not avoid the cracks in the sidewalk because they would break
my mother's back.
They would crack mine. I knew this for certain, the way
a driver feels the creep of another car on her tail and knows
she is about to be slammed into.
Some secrets I cannot divulge:
Watching the clock at midnight will set tragedy in motion.
Confessing to the smallest infraction results in banishment.
I do not admit to belief in superstitions.
The commandment against boasting is a precaution
against the evil eye, who waits to snatch babies.
The 9th of *Av* a fast day to keep away further horrors.
The golem can rise again, his protection so fleeting.
The danger of a friend turning against you as real
as a disease invading the body, once you name it aloud.

Kresty Prison

St. Petersburg, Russia

Twenty-five years ago, a battalion of arms
thrust through window slats,

slicing the air in stylized formations, a prisoners'
Morse Code to the lovers, parents, children,

who congregated in front of my apartment building.
Tiny cones scribbled with messages inside sailed

over the street in an arc like an assault of arrows.
These the only means of communication.

No visitors allowed in the remand prison,
built in the shape of a cross 150 years ago.

Political prisoners and common thieves
crammed together—20 to a cell

designed for solitary confinement.
Soviet law ordained six to a cell

but no officials followed the rules
and none do now either.

Wracked with TB, the prisoners sleep in shifts
on three-level bunk beds and the floor.

My first time in that apartment rented from a friend,
who did not warn me of these Saturday night

disturbances or the danger of the neighborhood,
I was awoken at 3 a.m. by shouts below my window

that bounced across to the prison and wafted
over the Neva and out to sea.

I've been back to Russia many times since.
Lived in that apartment twice, until I too

became callous to the inmates.
They closed the prison finally, real estate now

more valuable: they're building a luxury hotel
in that spot, the new jail outside the city limits

where prisoners can still be held indefinitely.
Families trek there on weekends, desperate

for news, any news, but no one listens.

DDR Museum

Berlin, Germany

Meandering along the River Spree on a scorching day,
we stumble into a line stretching along the embankment,
like in Soviet days, join it, when a block-long queue meant
something good for sale, even if when you got to the front,
the shoes were brown, manmade, size 48 and you wore a 40.
You'd buy anyway for a friend or to sell on the black market.

The 200th anniversary of Karl Marx prompts this trip,
my husband reverential to the socialist monuments in Berlin.
I'm more skeptical, having travelled alone as a 17-year-old
in the USSR; later lived in post-Soviet Russia in the aftermath
of shortages, no customer service, a lingering fatalism
that makes people resistant to real change.

But here we are, joining the other tourists.
"Love, Sex & Socialism," a temporary exhibit.
The historic photo of Brezhnev kissing Honecker, 1979,
in front of the ticket counter.
"Cash or credit card," the clerk asks.

Visitors of all ages will want to join in the fun, a sign in English says.
Interactive games, a fresco "In Praise of Communism."
Take a seat in an original Trabant P601 for a simulated drive!
Children can explore an East German kindergarten room,
complete with plastic play dishes and utilitarian cots, nothing so different.
A photo of children in striped pajamas (reminiscent of
concentration camp uniforms), sitting, pants down, on long
"potty benches, a first step to social education."

The other tourists laugh and joke, cross over to an
"Authentic reconstruction of a high-rise apartment with five rooms,"
stroke the quaint flowered curtains of the kitchen,
swing open its cupboard doors to peer at baking soda,
porcelain mixing bowls, similar to a Western apartment.

Then march into an office, lift the receiver of the rotary phone
on a large wooden desk, devoid of photos, devoid of anything else.

Maybe I just don't have a sense of humor.
We too wander room to room, snicker at the aerobics videos
of dancers with smiles too wide, dressed in white Go-Go boots and
matching glittery minidresses, swinging their arms to disco music,
heads helmeted by hairsprayed coifs.

I want to ask someone why there is no exhibit
of Hohenschönhausen Prison.
Of the Stassi pulling men from their apartments.
Female Olympic swimmers fed steroids,
not understanding why their bodies changed.
The 140 men and women who tried to climb over,
tunnel under the Wall and died in the effort.

Instead we cross into the gift shop where
I pick up a piggy bank of Marx's head,
turn it over to check the price.
Country of origin: China.

A Student Says Everything We Read Is Depressing

So I point out the crisp sheets under the dead body,
how the autumn leaves crunched underfoot, even as
one man pressed the muzzle of a gun to the other's back.
I would like to draw the student's attention to the tourist's plaid shorts,
the dark socks with his sandals. Haven't we all seen this?

Once in the Soviet Union, traveling by myself at age eighteen,
when most Americans didn't think that was even possible,
I ate in a hotel restaurant. Most everything on the menu
was met with a *nyet*. Still I couldn't believe my good fortune
to be here in this country whose literature I loved.

At a table close to mine sat an American couple, Texan (I guessed).
The man, speaking to his wife in a tone much too loud, said,
*I can accept some things, but I saw Brezhnev kiss another man
right on the lips!* I only hoped the waitress did not speak English;
I certainly pretended I didn't.

Next day on a train chugging towards the cities of
the Golden Ring, a stranger presented me
with an orange, an expensive gift. My Russian was not good,
but I still remember the fragrance of that fruit, so hard to come by
in a Soviet winter. The sweetness of it.

On the 150th Anniversary of the Homestead Act

Go West was the cry, and west they came.
Beckoned by advertisements plastered on walls
and on two-page newspaper spreads.
Pretty girls with baskets brimming with oranges.
Land so rich, you could reach your hand in
and pull out vegetables full grown.
The railroad posters practically guaranteed it!

President Lincoln signed the Homestead Act
in 1862. Within reach: 160 acres for each person
willing to build a house, plant and live there five years.
Man. Woman. Married. Single. White. Black.
(Though fewer blacks received land.)

Just after midnight, Daniel Freeman,
Union scout in the Nebraska Territory, persuaded
a clerk at a New Year's Eve party to unlock
the land office so he could file the first claim.
Soon waves of newcomers flooded the Great Plains.
The lure of land impossible to ignore.

Farmers sought fertile ground; others fled
slavery and ten-hour shifts in textile mills.
Families bumped along in wagons, men on horseback.
From Europe too they flocked: Swedes and Germans,
Czechs and Russians, until almost half of Nebraska
was claimed.

Corn displaced tallgrass; wheat thrust aside
shortgrass. On land with few trees, sod houses called
soddies were erected. Solid structures, though
 in rainstorms, the roofs of pots had to protect the soup.

Nature is never to be trusted.
Drought. Blizzards. Tornadoes. Fire. Locusts.
Some people abandoned the punishing conditions,
moved on, fanning out to Colorado,
Idaho, New Mexico, California.
All told 30 states: 10% of America settled.

      Born in a homestead state on this western shore,
I am a grandchild of immigrants. Like generations
before, my parents succumbed to the siren call
of the unknown, packing their small car in New York,
driving seven days west. They traded the Atlantic
for the Pacific where my own children were born.

      I drive into Nebraska for the first time.
An August thick with moisture. The sun searching
for its seat in a cloudless sky; below, the bluestem
leans into a faint breeze. At dusk wild turkeys
chastise their young beside the creek. Cicadas
crank up their choirs as the light dims.

      Midsummer, the prairie awash with the yellow
of coneflower, pink of foxglove, purple of thistle.
The switchgrass thick as veins, tough as settlers.
A common grackle alights onto the top of an oak
and begins to trill.

Listening to a Russian Band Play Dave Brubeck

My eye wanders off the four-lane highway.
Corn on my right, soy on my left.
I'm looking for roadside shrines, though I can't say why.
Once on the Karelian Peninsula, an area
that switched back and forth, Finland to Russia,
I came upon an icon at an unmarked crossroads
sheltered in a tiny hut with a carved eave.
In winter, sparrow families would seek refuge
there from snow blasting in from the Baltic.
Sometimes a candle burned before an icon
of Saint Nikolai, patron of travelers.

In Los Angeles the shrines rise on sidewalks
beside the scene of an accident: Mexican saint candles
in tall glasses, a balloon bouquet, handwritten notes
clipped to the ears of teddy bears.
I drive further.
On the radio, someone shouts out *James Bond*
and the band jumps into a speeding melody.
After solos on the violins and keyboard,
a Yuri, Kiril and Alex are introduced.
A concert in Lincoln, Nebraska, though it's unclear
if the musicians live here or are on an American tour.
The highway edges over a gentle slope.
Clouds tighten into a darkening fist.
A whirlpool of sparrows funnels over the field.

II.

An Answer for Everything

Only my 2nd time in Siberia, so I cannot
say if the -18°C. today is usual or not.
All around people walk to buy groceries
or wait for the morning tram.

Sidewalks not brushed clean these past
8 days, the official new year's holiday.
A sheen of ice slicks the walkways
like a child's face in need of scrubbing.

I have been thinking about string theory.
How to explain the universe, yes
the pull of gravity, but its opposite too,
an electromagnetic force attracting then repelling.

If only the world were so easily explained:
Last year's rains in California,
followed by an explosion of new
growth in the forests.

We marveled at the green stubble
on the hills of the Sepulveda Pass,
usually parched a dull brown.
Reassured ourselves the drought was over.

But summer fires more ferocious than ever
tore through cities usually inured,
then intensified in late fall, persisting
even into winter months.

16 hours into the future,
on the other side of the world,
I gaze into the dark
of a Siberian morning.

My phone pings with photos of home,
where rain is unleashing hillsides.
The earth, long parched, gives way
pulling down houses and everything in its path.

On the Trans-Siberian Railway

I

The land rises steeply around the train.
Even the birches appear starved in winter.
The sun fights through a colorless sky
casting anemic shadows as if
hundreds of bony fingers all pointed
in the same direction.
Four hours on the Trans-Siberian in winter,
the train chugging past fists of tiny
villages choked by snow,
plumes of smoke rising.

II

I am silent.
Not the usual fear of a foreign woman
travelling alone overnight in a berth
for four. It is daytime, the compartments
without doors and I sit across from
a woman and her small child who does not
stop talking for six hours.
Outside, 200 kilometers of snow and birch.
The mother pulls food from bags:
meat, potatoes, sweets, offering me nothing.

These are not the Russian trains I remember
from decades ago where sausages, black bread
and vodka were passed passenger to passenger,
a guitar pulled magically from under a bunk,
mournful melodies escaping through
many doors, neither language nor suspicion ever an obstacle.

Presentation

The cat parades outside in the rain
marching up and down the patio,
black coat slicked down like the Mafioso
who leaned against the hoods
of Benzes in our neighborhood
in St. Petersburg, waiting for their bosses
to emerge from a prerevolutionary building.
A floozy hangs from their arms:
peroxide-blonde, huge fake earrings, enough
cleavage to embarrass my children.
At first they were afraid, having seen, even then,
enough old movies to recognize gangsters.
But these men were not interested
in the likes of us. They had bigger fish to catch,
expat businessmen to shake down, a government
official to photograph in the public baths
with a woman (not his wife) packed on either side,
a wide grin on his red puckered face.
We walked quickly by the men on Marat St.,
the English silenced on our tongues. Why tempt fate?
We knew pockets were secreted with silencers,
how a pedestrian was nothing more than an inconvenience
caught under a shower of bullets, all an unfortunate
mistake. Timing is everything.

Russian Chocolates

I never knew I had patriotism until I moved to Russia.
Now I fight the urge to justify all the things I criticized back home.
The apartment building staircase reeks of urine.
Communal space is not valued here.
Cigarette butts mound in the lobby.
Piles of dirty snow line the street.
Why can't you camp wherever you want to in America?
a fellow instructor in Ulan-Ude asks.

We wait to be rescued by the bell.
So many topics we cannot understand about one another:
how I wanted my children to go away for university,
how she will decide her children's careers.

My Siberian colleagues like it when I recite
all I love about Russia, but suspicious too.
They perceive life in the U.S. is easier.

What is your background?
Living in Russia, I am often asked this question.
In America, a code for
You don't really belong here. This is not your home.

Here men from the Caucuses are yanked from the metro
escalator by police demanding their papers.
Back home men and women of color are pulled over while driving.
On a tram the other day a young man yelled at my landlady to
go back to Israel, a country she has never been to.
I used to think that would never happen in America,
but that was then.

On a break between classes, someone has set out a plate
of cookies and Russian chocolates
wrapped in brightly decorated foil,
put the kettle on for tea.
This ritual so important, civilizing.

Occupying the Body

Moving into someone else's house is like occupying a body.
You recognize it as human but the clothes don't quite fit.
The voice leaking from your throat croaks with words
you would never use.

This rust-colored kitchen has horizontal windows
slightly larger than the slits in castle walls.
More like the eyebrows of metal filings we'd slash with a magic
wand onto Wooly Willy, that cartoon face from our childhoods.

Plates and bowls stack on an open shelf; various-sized glasses
huddle on a wire rack nudging one another;
school children bunched for a class photo.
You can tell this is not earthquake country.

I wander room to room, feeling for light switches.
Investigating this new body to see if I am just a squatter,
a dybbuk forcing her way in,
waiting to fly out when the time is right.

Backyard Alchemy

He dug and dug, unearthing garbage
from a dump by the creek.
An old fuse, beer cans, a car jack.
Going for the big kahuna, he said.
He'd stir it, believing in a kind of alchemy.
Copper—like a man with body and soul.
Iron—in his blood, in the Virginia
clay of this red land.
Tunneling into the past a surgical
procedure to excavate the detritus:
washers, lawnmower blades, metal,
as if the scraps could be reassembled
into a Golem, life created from dust,
a second chance for these hills.
In the story, the Golem grows bored,
turns on the people it's charged to protect.
Hadn't this community too been betrayed before?
Suited officials who arrived in fancy cars,
promising jobs, money to support their families.
Later, the earth gouged, the miners' lungs blackened.
Now no food or prospects.
The man peeled off sheaths of wiring until
three smaller wires are stripped naked for veins.
This has got to be good for something.

Pilgrimage

For over a year I've passed this makeshift shrine.
Carnations, always fresh, though their number varies,
unlike in Russia where even numbers are for the dead,
odd for the living. You have to count the stems of flowers
carefully before each purchase.

I've memorized that face, his photo pinned to the tree.
Could pick it out in a lineup: dark gelled hair,
tawny skin, mischievous smile.
With only a headshot, I don't know his height,
can only guess his age at early 20s.

This road I drive weekly.
Beige apartment buildings crowd together like sentries.
Too embarrassed to stop to read the sign propped against
the flower bucket, the saint's candle in front of a city magnolia.

The worry about my youngest living in a hillside yurt,
so forgetful she drives without a license.
My mother died before Rosh Hoshanah.
I wonder if she looks over the yearly list: who shall live and who shall die.
Surely she could have rejected that young man's name,
pleaded to give him more years.
And his mother who survived him, renewing
the red and yellow carnations, as cars speed by to catch that flight
to take them far away from this city of palms and waves.

Hummingbirds Fighting

Sparks of beauty
in this year of crippling drought.

Summoned outside
by a series of clicks, I assumed insects:
cicadas or another invader seeking water.
Instead, a hummingbird in attack,
dive bombing a Black-Chinned
attempting to land on the feeder.

All day the Rufous, glowing like an orange coal,
zipped out of nowhere pinpointing
the plastic flowers.

The hummingbird retracts its tongue
squeezing nectar into the mouth. Squinting, I believed I witnessed that too.

I tried to provide respite,
a perch to save their energy, but
when the Rufous chased the Anna, I shooed it away.
A futile attempt at equality.

Dismantle the feeder?
Rewarding pettiness seems wrong.

I wanted to believe in nature.
Something steady to hang on to as the world slips.

But who can resist those acrobats hovering as if on breath, slowing the spinning globe.

Crow in Winter

His beak is stuck in the snow
like a bomber that went down
in an air show.
Wings outstretched, as if the crow
expected to lift off once again.
Sadness sweeps over me
as I gaze out the apartment
window painted with
new year's messages.
What is it about the death
of this bird that strikes me so?
The loneliness of living 16 hours
ahead of everyone I know,
never mind this is my choice.
The black and white world
of a Siberian winter so harsh
even a crow cannot survive.

Defending the Prairie

You can't love the mountains if you don't love the prairie,
the minister's daughter proclaims, leaning back
in the luncheonette booth.

Books and grasses are what she loves most.
A slight edge when she recounts visitors'
dismissal of these flat fields, as if height overrules all.

The Chassids believe the world is recreated each moment.
The chipping sparrow's trill bounces from box elder to bur oak
as the cardinal's two-syllable call, thumps a base line.

The light shifts looking for refuge, hooking
in the bluestem; shadows shrink as the sun hurries
to settle its body for the night. Air cooling,

the meadowlark tests its lungs.

Shivaree

Noise can scare away the devil,
but why invoke it as a blessing?
Even now in Nebraska at dusk on a wedding day
the townspeople march to the newlyweds' home,
beating tin oyster cans, ringing cow or sleigh bells
until the young couple emerges from their post-
ceremony cocoon to invite the rowdy crowd in.

The groom tries to placate the young men with cigars,
as the bride cuts ever widening slices of pie.
Sometimes the parties get out of hand, a bride made
to stand on the driver's side fender, the groom on
the passenger's, forced to hold hands across the hood
to keep from being thrown off. Danger the tune
carried toward a successful marriage.

I know enough to sing while hiking, though
the morning a mountain lion stood feet away on
my back porch, no melody protected me.
Neither of us moved or spoke.
Perhaps the startled silence saved us both.

Driving on Hwy. 31

Rounding a bend, it wasn't the black ice
that startled me from tedium, but the white church

perched on the hillside, no road, no driveway, no trees.
Just scrub low to the ground, bleached of color.

No cross on its roof bearing the promise of heaven.
No sign declaring its allegiance.

Abandoned by the mother church
or too few locals to support it?

Its pastor lured to a city where pews can fill,
a flock to follow his sermons.

The front façade, a ghostly presence.
Not even a handle on its double doors.

Can a person ever find salvation?

A cardboard cutout, its generations of stories
locked inside or thrust out,

strewn across this desolate two-lane highway,
as lumber trucks roar by, scattering pebbles in their wake.

Licorice Fern

i.

Leaves are falling from the maple and black cottonwood,
a rain of green so beautiful I forget

it's because of the drought.
The alder cannot hold onto its little serrated boats.

I start to count types of ferns: sword fern, lacy,
licorice. An epiphyte on the branches of

bigleaf maples: they say this fern will survive
even if the moss dries, rehydrating after winter rains.

We think they are delicate, but fine-toothed fronds can
propel like weapons from the hands of children.

ii.

Now the calling of birds: flicker, creeper, nuthatch.
Counting is habit forming, such certainty like the counting

of days of the Omer, the preparation and anticipation
of freedom: seven weeks, forty-nine days between the redemption

from slavery and receiving of the Torah. There is too much
to remember: why must we be responsible for all the ills?

I have told you of the fire and ash, the sun fighting through
smoke to show its colors; now I wait for the fawn to discover

its face in the reflection pool and its mother to track her
two offspring, to keep them close, to let them wander.

III.

January

It is cold
I am in Siberia
Why should I be surprised

The temperature does not fall
Too cold for such sudden movement
It inches downward, always and only

in one direction
At 2 a.m. I could not sleep
Looking out the window

mounds of snow seemed to pulse
as if they needed to move
to stay alive

In the morning a blackbird pecked
along a bare branch
like hands feeling along

black and white keys
to coax out a melody
I used to think a man

crouched under a piano
hitting his little hammer
on the strings to release the notes

The bird gives up   flies away
They say the young are leaving Ulan-Ude
for Petersburg   for Moscow   abroad

What kind of life is left here
the steel factory closed
its great painted doors bolted

as if there were anything left inside
even the ghosts of Soviet bosses
have decamped to a Cyprus beach or

the fading boardwalks of Sochi
Before I left home last week
a man froze to death in Chicago

sitting on church steps   a porch
I don't remember
Think of the men who carried

down the rigid body
seated as if on a throne
or like the groom carried

on a chair at his wedding
and the poor bride
hanging on for dear life

grasping a white handkerchief
as her husband catches
the other end a symbol perhaps

of the fragility of marriage
No wonder Los Angeles
has the highest number of homeless

winters mild   rain now scarce
but further north fires
with voracious appetites

do not subside in autumn
No such thing as fire season anymore

Fairy Tale

[denial of truth] [statement of fact] Out of the jumble of horsetail and huckleberry a stag emerged, his antlers slick from morning rain. He stood motionless as a lawn decoration. [he was real] On another day clouded from wildfire smoke, outside the park, a stag [maybe the same, maybe not] was spotted. He froze where he was in the giant ferns, then turned and leapt away. It is true the three sons of a king were set impossible tasks to win the heart of the princess who had once been a white deer but that was a different story set between a mountain and a mine. On this island there is tearing down and building [it is not hard to figure out the villains] but the deer persist. Some people love them, others do not. [think destruction of rose bushes, beans, clover] There is rarely compromise between the two groups. A fawn was seen two days ago. The doe has not appeared. Whether this land is enchanted or not, no one can agree.

On Trying to Decide What Makes Me American

The ticket seller yells at my friend for buying two
regular tickets instead of one for a citizen, one for a foreigner.
How could she tell? I ask.

It is winter in Novgorod; in the brief daylight hours
we have come to tour St. Sophia Cathedral.
Black coat. Black boots. Black skirt.
Russian wool scarf with red flowers and fringe.
I am in total camouflage.
How did she know?
Your face, my friend says, *it's too open.*

In Paul Taylor's *Esplanade*
to Bach's Violin Concerto in E Major,
the dancers walk barefoot to the four corners of the stage.
Toe heel, toe heel, they turn decisively,
without the grace we are used to.
An arm flings back beckoning, speed picks up.
They run in a circle until one peels off,
leapfrogs over the others and lands each jump,
then skips off and begins again.
Something so American in these gestures, a confidence.

Does one learn optimism or is one born with it?
I, who was raised to be suspicious of happiness,
to always have purpose, and glance over my shoulder.
In Russia my face betrays me.
I shrug and pay the difference.

Waves

For days I think of waves:
bolts of heavy velvet in the fabric store's dusty backroom
where my father hunted for muslin to sew into the curtains
and bedspreads of my childhood, saving money
to pay for the house he built of felled redwoods

This week the Pacific throws 25-footers against the moorings of
Malibu Pier until they succumb to the battering

A surfer (ignoring warnings) drowns

Driven by my mother over the Bay Bridge, I pictured steel pylons
folding Origami-style, cars cascading like Tinker toys on a ramp

Engineers knew the challenges of building this bridge:
        high winds, inaccessible bedrock, an eight-mile span
Politicians were dubious until Herbert Hoover threw his support

After the Loma Prieta earthquake in 1989, repair crews affixed
an 18-inch troll secretly to the Bay Bridge, afraid their hard work would not be enough

A troll now guards the eastern span of the bridge. Wielding
an ironworker's mallet and torch, he waits for the next rumble
or waves to rise up
and swallow us all

Little Odessa

Wave it was called—first, second, third.
Brezhnev inched the door open and Jews fled,
many to this section of Los Angeles.

Now the old neighborhood is being taken over—
a pot shop, a designer sneakers store.
Old Russian Jews pull shopping carts,
mumbling words: loss, homesick, *toska* (yearning)
Latin terms of herbs that grow only in Siberia,
Ukraine or the dacha garden left behind.

Their children, born here, have moved away
with vans crammed with furniture, flat screens bought new,
things they cannot live without in their tract homes
in gated suburbs of the San Fernando Valley.

They visit on holidays that in a generation will be
forgotten: Red Army Day, Victory Day, Nov. 7,
even if they remember Yom Kippur and Passover.
American holidays too, of sun and beach and bounty,
the parents' tables sag with foods of their childhoods:
pelmeni, salad Olivier, salted dried fish.

Where will these delicacies be found once this
stretch of store fronts disappear, swallowed up
by slick bars with repurposed farmhouse beams as if
authenticity could be bought at prices never imagined.

Understanding a Language

I thought if I only concentrated
enough I could understand any language.
A delayed reaction, the way a spice
breaks through a sauce after the first swirl in the mouth.

Some words drop hard and break
into chunks of iceberg; others dissolve as they slide
back on the tongue.
Maybe this foolishness was the same as wishing for
the answer to a math problem

or the legacy of years spent as an American child
in non-English speaking countries where
old women would grab at my curls, twirl them
around their fingers and coo or spit
phrases I could not decipher.

Can the mourning dove years later
recognize the bird it nested in the hanging fern
if their paths crossed in the eucalyptus
bordering the park?
Did the stick figures I'd will to prance
off the page, bulk up with pecs and fists to pay
back the bullies who tortured us?

A cluster of students gossip and flirt
in the hallway. Turkish maybe? I linger
on the fringes of their orbit. If their
gravitational pull sucks me in, I'll get
their joke, the guys doubled over,
laughing so hard, it hurts.

Of Magic and Superstition

One should not believe in superstitions,
but still it is best to be heedful of them. – Sefer Chassidim

1. Sorcery

Many accused Jews of sorcery,
Jewish physicians of poisoning their patients:
a man who recovered proved the point;
the one who died, certified it.

Is it better to be thought harnessing black magic and
have it validated through restored health or to fail
and have the black magic confirmed?

An impenetrable language does not shield a community
from attacks, nor does huddling behind locked doors.

2. The Name

A man's name is the essence of his being. – Sefer Tziyoni

Naming a child stamped it with the character of its
previous owner; the choice fraught with possibility and danger
for the previous soul could be transported into the body of the infant.

It was forbidden to name a child after a living parent.
If the Angel of Death slips in to claim a parent,
he might snatch the baby instead, robbing it of its life.
Such was the danger.

Or the soul of a dead ancestor could forsake
its heavenly home and reenter the realm of the living.

If misfortune slapped a man, a baby must not be given
the same name, as bad luck would follow the child.

Be careful too in the spelling of a name.
Magic demands adherence to a form,
even syllables, that little family of sound, is potent.
Consonants, the body, vowels, its garments.

3. The Magic of Words

I will bring you out; I will redeem you – Exod. 6:6

Words hidden in the bible can save or doom a person.
T'hillim, recited before sleep, guarantees
a person will wake in the morning.
Reciting a psalm that spells out a city's name
protects a community from harm and evil spirits.

Sometimes it is necessary to read each word in a verse
backwards; then the whole verse this same way. Repeating
this will weave a protective curtain that will fool evil, chase it away.

Words can be whispered over water, be written on the skin
of an apple, even on a hard-boiled egg, then consumed to open
the heart. Charms against forgetfulness can be chanted.
Each letter employed to protect, to ward off, to bring forth.

4. Amulets

Write them on the doorposts of thy house and upon thy gates – Deut. 6:9

A man born with a caul must keep it with him through his life
to protect against demons who battle during a storm.

Hanging an afikomen in the house or sheltering it in a pouch
will guard against evil men and evil spirits.

Place a notched straw under the tongue to receive a fair hearing.

Wrap a sprig of fennel in silk with coins and wheat,
seal it with wax and recite an incantation.

A chamsa placed in a crib will ward off the evil eye.

To this day, we mount them as much to protect as to declare.

Adorn an amulet with magical figures, the number five.

All this calls forth blessings we pretend not to believe.

Evangelical Church

Schooled in England fifty years ago, I can recite
The Lord's Prayer and *Psalm 23* by heart.
When they found out I was Jewish, I was dismissed
from chapel but not from mandatory religion class.

I've been in churches before, so this evangelical
service in Russia was both familiar and foreign
with its surge of syrupy pop tunes praising Jesus against
a background slideshow of swaying palm trees.
A sub-zero storm blew the snow sideways.

Theologically it could have been Kansas or Texas,
except the language was wrong and the building
was unmarked for safety; non-Orthodox churches
are under state attack, accused of brainwashing and
seducing Russians away from their one true religion.

Thin men slipped into the pews.
Their elongated faces full of suffering,
like penitents in an icon.
I couldn't stop staring at their knuckles
tattooed with a thief's cross or a winged arrow.

The congregants were friendly, pointing out
page numbers so I could follow along.
After, in the church basement, I was offered Mongolian
dumplings, embarrassed to turn them down, as I don't eat pork.

My colleague asked in English (so no one would understand),
whether I noticed anything about the men.
I demurred, unwilling to answer and risk offending.
Was this a test?

They're ex-convicts recently released.
Converted in prison, he said.
My mind races to Dostoevsky and Solzhenitsyn.
My background to this world.

I knew where the gulags had been.

The Air is Full

The air is full of particles,
ash from the smoke of fires to the north

Last night the sky an ungodly color
shifting orange to yellow and back

A kind of stillness that in California
means earthquake, whether it arrives or not

*

In the dream a man stood up.
Nothing unordinary about him,
except for the half circle of people
(I hesitate to call them disciples)
He raised his hand   Sparks flew

I have never succumbed to full acceptance
even as I envy those who can follow
without questioning: the Amish boy
in Shipshewana, who rejects the tractor
in favor of plow horses in the field,
the Chassidic woman who handed over her son
to be circumcised, not hiding in the bedroom as I did

*

It is true that God was put on trial at Auschwitz
He did not fare well

*

I was taught how to question
not how to believe

*

We are told there were two sets of tablets
one destroyed, one saved
Fire and cloud

*

We are always carving a new golden calf
searching for solace to convince ourselves
we chose right

*

I scratch out letters from branches
the aleph bet in the three languages
I pretend to know
Compare their shapes, assess their durability

*

The flakes thicken, carpeting the meadow
coating prairie flax and cornflower
I look upward but no prayer is answered

Madame X

after John Singer Sargent

Her face in profile, raised eyebrow, tightened mouth, dainty nose.
An impossibly tiny waist envied by women over many continents.
Right hand grips the table's edge, as if she would topple
without holding on to it. Left firmly clutches a fan.
The scandal of bare shoulders, a plunging neckline.
The black velvet bodice a shield daring the viewer to linger.
In the artist's first version, the jeweled strap of her dress
slides off her shoulder, but is this the problem or the woman's
brazen challenge of sex and money to bourgeois life?
After the first exhibition, Singer pulled up the strap.

Madame X, daughter of Creole parents in New Orleans.
Her mother begged for loans to take her daughter
to Europe to snare a husband.
Paris seemed a dream after the Civil War.
She was a beauty but unconventional, a flutter of men
drew to her as helpless as moths to a flame,
"stalking her as one does a deer."
She struggled, deemed unworthy by the highest echelons.
Her painter, too, was waiting for his big break.
Savaged by the critics, who compared her portrait's
skin tone to that of a corpse.
We have forgotten the other painters rewarded in that Salon.
Madame X reigns over the gallery.
Immortal, finally, imperious as she wished.

Ball in Columbia

after Fernando Botero

Even dancing the tango, the couple's arms stay stiff,
resting on the other's. Clothing does not twist
with motion, no sweaty embrace, no desire,
no night of passion.
Dots and dashes on the small rectangle of dance floor,
cigarettes and apples (oranges?).
Naked bulbs hang like fireflies in the air but
are strangely immobile and do not give out enough
light or warmth to keep the dancers going.
The six men in the band nearly identical,
same soft felt hat, the downward arrow
of a pencil moustache, circle of chin.
They play instruments, a bass with no strings,
a guitarrón, but they are not an ensemble.
even if we lean in and listen attentively.
If there is a melody line, we can't hear the notes.

Another Winter in St. Petersburg

A man stepped off the embankment
        onto the ice
The river was not reliable
        but he trusted it
the way a couple plunges into love
        not knowing if it will last
February, the ice could crack under foot
        not surprising anyone
Assuredly he walked with certainty
        a kind of belief
He did not need an answer to know
        his prayer reached its destination
The wind swirled, tossing a confetti of snow
        onto the broad back of the river
He continued until out of sight
        Scouring the papers the next day
no mention of a man sliding under
        though over many nights
I saw one leg, then the other, his torso
        swallowed too, silently
as if nothing had happened

Half a World Away

She won't let me take a picture of them before I leave

I was instructed   she said   *by a shaman*

not until he's twelve   *a danger*   *death*

I don't understand   Is there such a thing   this power?   The soul leaving the body

when the image forms in the shutter?

A mother and son

The boy designated an invalid

so home-schooled   Nothing visible   but he's flighty   building jet

airplanes from balsa   Hunched over the skin of wood cutting

a Tupolev-134   an Antonov-12

until the wings form and spread   A man sits in Row 12B waiting for his dinner

The day I arrived   Timur age 9   put on his Russian Navy hat

Prompted by his mother   finally said hello

One month later   I left at 3 a.m.   Never got to say goodbye   Emptied
my pockets of rubles

piled on the kitchen table   No use for them at home   Maybe

she'll buy him wheels for the jet   a tractor-trailer to haul it to the hangar

I wanted a photo I never got

IV.

Reduced to Black and White

A worker in orange overalls
scrapes his shovel
against snow and ice
until a rectangle forms,
neat as a cemetery plot.
I wonder how they bury people
in winter with the ground
as unforgiving of the dead
as to the living.
Outside the taste of wood smoke
on the tongue
from villages ringing this city.

I disembark at the university
beneath the gaze of Lenin,
a great stone head sculpted
with Buryat eyes.
Statues pulled down
all over Russia, curious
that this head still stands,
bodiless, thousands
of miles from Moscow.
This morning he wears
a skullcap of snow.
One eyebrow brushed
white as if questioning
why he must endure
sub-freezing temperatures.

After all he did for this country,
doesn't he deserve
to lay his tired head
somewhere green,
somewhere tropical

without regret,
not frozen all winter
while politicians
argue about his role,
rewriting his fate
this way or that.

Below Zero, the Temperature Falling

Starting two days ago, I was warned of the approaching cold:
-25°C today, tomorrow -31°C, -40°C Saturday.

I cannot imagine such temperatures, how others live here,
go about their days working, walking to the store.

This morning I watched a toddler on the bus, a muffler
wrapped over its mouth. Never could determine boy or girl.

The child, bundled in snow suit, boots and fur hat
clasped a little sand shovel in mittened hands.

Grip tight as if by holding on, the toddler could
will itself to a beach, a sandbox, strip off

the clothing and dig and dig.
Three weeks in Siberia and my world shrinks.

The delight of a hot lunch in the cafeteria,
a fatalistic shrug when the internet won't work at the university.

I abandon plans to go to a museum, walk carefully
so as not to fall on the slick sidewalk, the snow

stinging as it's flung by the wind.
I cannot remember when I arrived nor when I am leaving.

In the Scheme of Things

The roof is leaking
through a light fixture

Grateful for rain after a scorched summer

My daughter has not called for months
texts unanswered I want to send again and again

She gives away all she has, collects food to distribute

A bill for $450   Did we leave the lights on all night?
Use more than our allotment of water?

We both have jobs, paychecks

The new cat has disappeared
how can I tell its former owner?

My husband's spine is behaving

Rosh Hoshanah, I break open a pomegranate
spill its seeds over the counter, swoop them into my palm

their juice runs through my fingers

Staining red everywhere it flows

Apprentice Shaman

Days she works in a Soviet-era factory,
      the lathe creaky as if it had arthritis.
Her thick fingers not as nimble as they once were
      but nights she studies with a Buryat shaman
to prepare for her real work.
      If the universe is divided into three worlds—
the upper, the earth, the underworld,
      that day on the banks of Lake Baikal,
the apprentice shaman hovered among them.
      Trees hung with ribbons,
red for supplication to the sun spirits, green
      to protect nature, blue for spirits of the sky.
We stood on a bank that jutted over the water.
      Waves of ice were frozen mid-motion,
sharp as incisors in the sub-zero cold,
      a blue so bright it hurt the eyes.
Holding a drum-tambourine to her chest,
      she beat and chanted to summon the spirits.
That night, we lay on cots in the one-room cabin.
      A growl escaped her lips as if a Siberian wolf
were trapped inside. Threatening or protecting,
      I did not know which.

If Prayer Were Another Form of Superstition

In one window, a man or mannequin
sprawled on a couch, legs outstretched.
A replica of a village in another
like a diorama rising from a shoebox.
The structures were brick, turn of the century.

She did not question how she ended up on the street
or why a tiger was following her, its colors muted.
Possibly it was harmless.
The fear thrilling because she was not sure this was real.

Maybe it was and the good genes she inherited
protected her, as they had her father when he missed
the flight out of O'Hare that later crashed, with no survivors.
There was the time a bombing shattered the metro
she commuted on daily in Russia but fortunately
she no longer worked at that institute.

Spared again but worried, she started a list
of the near misses, claiming not to believe in luck or fate.
This was a lie.
If prayer were another form of superstition, she would pray.

In Siberia, I Watch My Host

Ilya sits at the kitchen table,
open bottle of beer before him,
pours half a glass, dips a finger in,
taps it on the tabletop.
For the house spirits, Marina
explains. To appease
or nourish, I am not sure,
nor what role the ancestors play.
In the Irkutsk Historical Museum,
a 19th c. shaman's robe hangs
with strips of metal and a few keys.
To summon the spirits
for protection or to banish evil ones.
I think of our own Passovers,
finger dipping in the wine and tapping.
Blood. Vermin. Locusts.
The power. The fear.

It Is Even Colder in Irkutsk

I no longer understand numbers.
-22°C, -32°C, what's the difference?

Branches covered in a sheen of white,
fingers slicked in a second skin.
A breeze barely audible
shudders twigs and snaps icicles.

It's not that Siberians don't get cold,
they say, *but that they know how to dress.*
Sable. Mink. Black Persian lamb.
Fur hats round as kitchen knobs
perch on women's heads.

Yesterday at a lecture the other women
wore muted shades: gray, lavender, beige.
Why, when this Siberian world must
crave color to survive the long winter?
The Angara River that slices Irkutsk
is frozen, though fisherman cut holes
to catch the prized omul, even in January.
How strange it will be to return to
California, the temperature rarely
dipping below 50°F.
Where I am often cold.

After Watching Russian Grandmothers
Sing Leonard Cohen's 'Hallelujah'

Well I've heard there was a secret chord
That David played and it pleased the Lord

Seven women, aproned, hair covered in fringed kerchiefs
(we used to call babushkas), all in plaid blouses, oldest
so short she barely reaches the others' shoulders,
her smile impish, as if she's hiding something.
Their first refrain stiff, voices gravelly, but
by the final chorus, they form a unit, arms woven.

When I brought American students here, how I wanted
them to fall in love with Russia as I had. Not to ignore
the repressive regime, its control of the press, but to savor
blini with wild mushrooms, to bend over tangled bushes of
red currants, pluck the berries and plunk them into a rusted bucket.
To wander this vast country beyond its museums and palaces.

Now, in Los Angeles a year later, after an urgent text to meet up,
a student from the trip slips into a booth, slides her cell phone
across the table. This ringleader, always cracking jokes,
silent as she watches me pick up the phone.

Another student from the group stands with four women,
their naked bodies barely concealed by large feathers.
A porn star now. That night, sleepless, I scroll through photos
from the trip, looking for clues. Not her plumped lips and
enhanced breasts (yes I had missed that) but a reason for
this change that eludes me, and how I had failed her.

In a spring blizzard we placed flowers at Tchaikovsky's grave,
tucked a carnation into an angel's hymnal.
The head of Pan snow-capped, eyes closed, fingers
playing his pipe, heralding the passage to heaven.
Russia had saved me. Why did it not save her too?

Driving to the Old Believer's Village

Over the Selenga River, leaving behind
a giant bronze sculpture of a Buryat woman,
arms draped with a Buddhist prayer shawl.
Past a tiger guarding the city, mouth wide
in a threatening snarl and pairs of leaping deer
on either side of the bridge.

At the end of the city, the last clusters of people
wait for a bus, stamping their feet in the
unforgiving cold, -22°C today.
The street now unpaved, small rocks kicked up by cars.
A truck stacked with huge logs struggles over a small incline.
To our left and right the land buried under more snow
than even Siberia has seen in decades.

In the back seat a young woman quietly sings
a mournful Russian folk song, a fitting accompaniment
to a landscape both bleak and beautiful.
Clusters of pines stand like tufts of hair on hilltops.
The road stretches endlessly until
the first wisps of smoke announce a village.
We turn off, greeted by a barking dog and wooden shutters
painted bright colors in this monochrome world.

Game of Chance

Think about the human spine
a ladder not meant to last

One night in Siberia
in a February that never lifted from darkness
even as the days expanded, I sat on the floor with
three women and one man, tossing
discolored pieces in a game of chance

I didn't know the Russian word
for vertebrae, did not recognize those clumps
as the bones of a horse, that beast crucial to the taiga

We cast and we counted
as the pile of bones rose and fell before each player

Isn't that what we want:
a sturdy backbone to hold us straight
no matter what is thrown our way?

Flags in a Time of Plague

Flags painted by children crisscross a small
front garden fecund with giant banana leaves
and poppies two feet high after a surprising April rain.
I want to scold the flags for not social distancing.
This morning a woman on her cell phone
did not see me and I yelled, I admit it,
afraid she would bump into me as I jogged by.
It feels like months and months confined,
when it's only six weeks, another eight until
the end of the semester and how can I possibly
grade all those papers, when all I want is
to collapse on the couch and watch movies?

A year ago January, I squished in a Jeep with
four Siberian colleagues for a drive to Lake Baikal.
Bare trees dotted the desolate road,
their branches strung with Tibetan prayer flags.
Bright blue *khatas* flapped in the wind.
The driver tossed coins from his window.
An hour later, we stopped to drop rubles
in the lap of a Buddha.
Now in Los Angeles, I unfurl a Buryat *khata*
out my apartment window,
pleading with it to bring compassion and calm,
both in short supply.

This Vine, That Country

The vine is strangling the orange tree.
Squeezing its branches.
This morning more unavoidable news
of the irrational president.
I spot the morning glory wrapped
around the metal pole that secures
the fence between unfriendly neighbors.
If a week goes by without ferocious yanking,
the vine sneaks up on another portion of green,
threatens to overtake a new corner of the garden.

Maybe I've grown intolerant.
Too many friends nudge and wink,
asking, *Is Putin my friend?*
Do I have any news?
since I have lived in Russia for long periods,
in his hometown. The irony of an imperial city
with its imposing palaces, art and ballet,
now famous as the birthplace of
the KGB president not lost on anyone.

A choice like that for an American,
a Californian even, bewilders them.
I am often at a loss to explain the pull.
I recognize it in other smitten Americans
who talk about Russia's raw beauty,
its literature and deep friendships
despite the corruption, troubling prejudices.
How we are still foreigners, regardless of the years there.
Maybe it's like this vine after all, a stubbornness.
No logic to it, just a persistence that refuses to die.

Glossary and Notes

Afikoman: A piece of matzoh that is broken in two during the Passover seder and set aside for children to find and then eaten at the end of the meal

Av: Eleventh month of the Jewish calendar

Chamsa: An ancient Middle Eastern amulet symbolizing the Hand of God. It is a protective sign and brings its owners happiness, luck, health and good fortune.

Dacha: A country cottage or house, common in the FSU (former Soviet Union)

Dybbuk: In Jewish folklore, a malevolent wandering spirit that enters and possesses the body of a living person, often causing mental illness; to get rid of it, the dybbuk has to be exorcized by a religious ceremony

Khata: A Tibetan prayer scarf, used in areas including Russia (Republic of Buryatia) and Mongolia

Rebbe: A rabbi, especially a religious leader of a Chassidic sect; in this case, refers to the Lubavitcher Rebbe, Rabbi Yosef Yitzchak Schneersohn

Sefer: A book, usually of Jewish religious literature

Shivaree: A noisy, often mocking serenade performed by a group of people to celebrate a marriage

Tania: Book of Chassidic mystical theology and psychology

T'hillim: Psalms

Most temperatures in the collection are noted in Celsius
  0 Celsius =   32 Fahrenheit
 -22 Celsius = -7.6   Fahrenheit
 -32 Celsius = -25.6 Fahrenheit

Acknowledgments

My gratitude to the editors of the journals in which poems first appeared, sometimes in different versions.

Apple Valley Review: "Another Winter in St. Petersburg"; "Driving to the Old Believer's Village, Siberia"

CCAR Journal: "Nursery Rhyme"; "Of Magic and Superstition"; Licorice Fern"

Catamaran: "Pilgrimage"

Crab Creek Review: "Apprentice Shaman"

December: "December, Russia"

Flash Flash Click Click: "On the Way to the Pushkin Hills"

Hawaii Pacific Review: "Reduced to Black and White"

Kitchen Table: "Half a World Away"

Museum of Americana: "Listening to a Russian Dave Brubeck"; "Defending the Prairie"; "Shivaree"; "February on the Horizon"

On the Seawall: "In Siberia, I Watch My Host"; "Russian Chocolates"

Patterson Literary Review: "Understanding a Language"

Pensive: "The Air is Full"

Poet Lore: "Game of Chance"

Prairie Schooner: "An Answer for Everything"; "It Is Even Colder in Irkutsk"; "January"; "This Vine, That Country"

Pratik: "Backyard Alchemy"

Salt: "Hummingbirds Fighting"

Sheila-Na-Gig: "Occupying the Body"; "Waves"

Southern Review: "A Student Says Everything We Read is Depressing"

Tampa Review: "White Nights"

Unearthed: "Driving Hwy. 31"; "Single Cell Scientist"

"In the Scheme of Things" in *101 Jewish Poems for the Third Millennium* (Ashland Poetry Press, 2021). "Nursery Rhyme" forthcoming in *Without a Doubt: Poems Illustrating Faith* (New York Quarterly Books, 2023). "On the 150th Anniversary of the Homestead Act" was commissioned by Homestead National Historical Park, National Park Service, 2011.

I am deeply grateful to Buryatia State University, Ulan-Ude, Russia, the inspiration for many of these poems and to my colleagues there. Thank you to the National Park Service and Homestead National Historical Park, to Surel's Place, Bloedel Reserve, and PLAYA, for artist residencies which enabled the writing of many poems. Gratitude to the Fulbright Foundation, which started me and continues to nurture me on this journey. A special thank you to Andrea Carter Brown who helped in immeasurable ways, and to Elena Baiartueva. To Mercedes Lawry, Antoinette Jaccard, Johanna Drucker, Saundra Woodruff, Norm Levine. In memory of Peggy Aylsworth Levine. To my family. Thank you to Kim Verhines, and Meredith Janning at SFASUP for giving this collection a home.

About the Author

Photo by David Berezin

Carol V. Davis is the author of *Because I Cannot Leave This Body* (Truman State Univ. Press, 2017) and *Between Storms* (TSUP, 2012). She won the 2007 T.S. Eliot Prize for *Into the Arms of Pushkin: Poems of St. Petersburg*. Her poetry has been read on National Public Radio, the Library of Congress and Radio Russia. Twice a Fulbright scholar in Russia, she taught in Siberia, winter 2018, and teaches at Santa Monica College, California and Antioch Univ. Los Angeles. She was awarded a Fulbright Specialist grant for Siberia in 2020, postponed because of Covid restrictions and now cancelled.

CPSIA information can be obtained
at www.ICGtesting.com
Printed in the USA
JSHW011836050223
37226JS00004B/18